This is also the stormiest workplace place on Earth. The icy winds can last for days. Blizzards are common and may cause whiteouts. During a whiteout, sometimes you cannot see more than a few feet in front of you.

This workplace is so remote that it isn't accessible by car. The only way in or out is by plane or ship.

Welcome to McMurdo Station, Antarctica.

A City in Antarctica

McMurdo Station is not just a workplace. It is a city. In fact, it is the largest city in Antarctica. It includes a harbor and a science station. It also includes three airfields and more than 100 buildings. The station has a bowling alley and a 9-hole golf course.

And, of course, McMurdo station has special buildings that keep people warm. More than 1,200 people live at the station in the summer. (Remember, you still have to wear heavy winter clothes in the summer.) In the wintertime (when it is really, really cold), fewer than 200 people live there.

McMurdo Station

by Phil Moschowitz

 HOUGHTON MIFFLIN HARCOURT
School Publishers

PHOTOGRAPHY CREDITS: **Cover** © GUY CLAVEL/AFP/Getty Images. **1** © Ann Hawthorne/CORBIS. **2-3** © Ann Hawthorne/CORBIS. **4** John McCombe/Getty Images. **5** © John Higdon/Age Fotostock. **6** Associated Press. **7** GUY CLAVEL/AFP/Getty Images. **8-9** Joseph Van Os/Getty Images. **10** Gordon Wiltsie/National Geographic/Getty Images. **11** C.J. Gilbert/OSF/Animals Animals-Earth Scenes. **12** Elaine Hood. **13** © CORBIS/Age Fotostock. **14** Danita Delimont/Alamy.

Printed in China

ISBN-13: 978-0-547-02141-6
ISBN-10: 0-547-02141-0

4 5 6 7 8 0940 18 17 16 15 14 13 12 11 10

The Coldest Workplace on Earth

This is the coldest workplace on Earth. Even on the warmest summer day, people wear heavy coats to go outside, as well as a hat and mittens. On the coldest winter day, the temperature might be 100 degrees below zero!

There are no stores at McMurdo Station. All of the food and equipment must be flown in or brought in by boat. Strong ships called icebreakers plow through the ice and break it up. After the ice is broken, supply ships can get through.

Airplanes with skis land on a special landing strip called a ski-way. Other planes, with wheels, land on a runway built on an ice shelf. This runway can be used during most of the year. During the warmest months, however, the ice begins to break up, and wheeled planes cannot land.

A Place to Do Research

Everyone visiting Antarctica must pass through McMurdo before heading to other places on the continent. Many scientists come through McMurdo to work on projects. Most of the other people traveling through McMurdo work to support the scientists. They include cooks, mechanics, and computer workers. Artists and writers also travel through as part of the Antarctic Artists and Writers Program.

McMurdo Station is a research facility. It is a place where scientists work. Some of the scientists at McMurdo Station study biology. Other scientists study stars and planets.

What Scientists Study at McMurdo Station

Antarctica is a great place to study the stars and planets. The air in Antarctica is very dry and cold. This makes it easier to see certain types of stars. Scientists have built a giant telescope near McMurdo Station.

Scientists also study Earth's climate from Antarctica. They send up large balloons and steer them into the clouds. These balloons have special instruments that give scientists information about the weather or how fast the wind is blowing.

Many scientists study the animals that live in Antarctica. These animals include whales, seals, fish, and penguins. However, the climate is too cold and windy for most animals and plants. Winter nights can last for months, and most plants die when there is no sun.

Many scientists at McMurdo study penguins. Penguins live partly on land and partly in the water. They do not build nests for their eggs. To keep an egg warm, the father penguin scoops it up onto his webbed feet. The mother penguin finds food.

The father penguin needs to take special care of the egg. Otherwise, it might slide away across the slippery ice. When the penguin chick hatches, it will call to its father with a whistle. The chick is hungry and needs to eat. So the mother needs to find food quickly. Soon the chick will grow into a junior penguin. It will then have a waterproof coat of feathers. Finally, the junior penguin will become an adult.

Scientists at McMurdo Station also study animals called krill. Krill look like shrimp. Krill are very important to the ecosystem in Antarctica. First, tiny fish eat the krill. Then seals and penguins eat the fish. Some seals, like the leopard seal, then eat the penguins. And killer whales eat the seals. This chain of animals would not survive without the tiny krill.

Wintertime at McMurdo Station

At McMurdo Station, most activity happens in the summer. In the winter, the weather is so extremely cold and stormy that it is hard to live there. No planes can fly in or out of McMurdo Station for six months.

Most people leave McMurdo Station in the wintertime. The people who don't leave spend most of their time inside. Because the weather is so cold, they might not go outside for weeks at a time. They can talk to their family and friends by phone or e-mail.

People at McMurdo Station work hard and have fun, too!

McMurdo Station is a remote outpost at the bottom of the world. It's very, very cold, but it's also an exciting and interesting place to work, with lots to study. It can be fun, too! Maybe someday you will have the chance to visit the coldest workplace on the planet!

Responding

✔ **TARGET SKILL** **Main Ideas and Details**

Scientists from all over the world work at McMurdo Station. What kind of work do they do? Copy the chart. List two details from the book that support the main idea.

Main Idea: Scientists study many things at McMurdo Station.

Detail: ?

Detail: ?

✏ Write About It

Text to World McMurdo Station is one of the coldest places on Earth. Write one paragraph describing a problem people might face living at McMurdo Station, and include a solution for the problem.

✔️ TARGET SKILL **Main Ideas and Details**
Tell important ideas and details about a topic.

✔️ TARGET STRATEGY **Infer/Predict** Use text clues to figure out important ideas.

GENRE **Narrative nonfiction** tells a true story about a topic.